—ST

2D-70x

17/

SURREY
COUNTY COUNCIL

Overdue items may incur charges
as published in the current
Schedule of Charges.

L21

Matador
9 Priory Business Park
Kibworth Beauchamp
Leicestershire LE8 0RX, UK
Tel: (+44) 116 279 2299
Fax: (+44) 116 279 2277
Email: books@troubador.co.uk
Web: www.troubador.co.uk/matador

ISBN 978 1783061 952

British Library Cataloguing in Publication Data.
A catalogue record for this book is available from the British Library.

Typeset in 11pt Aldine401 BT Roman by Troubador Publishing Ltd, Leicester, UK

YOU CAN & YOU MUST

Career Planning for Changing Times

Sue Liburd

"Looking all around and I'm watching the world, changing. Open up your eyes, you can see things rearranging."

Will.i.am

Welcome to YOU CAN & YOU MUST ~ an explorative look at five key principles essential for designing and managing your career in changing and turbulent times... because great careers don't just happen by chance.

Contents

Wake Up and Smell the Coffee

The world we inhabit is in transition. We are leapfrogging from the familiar to the new at an accelerated pace. We are in a time of big shifts, big change and rapid innovation, all of which means that the future is difficult to predict and is like a roller coaster to navigate. As a consequence, traditional approaches to career planning will no longer serve you. Forget carrying out a comprehensive skills and values audit based on the past, which you then utilise as a foundation to plan in detail your next career move. Forget designing a detailed long-term career plan marking out the steps that will take you to your desired career destination. That wisdom may have held true in periods of slow economic growth, for traditional careers of the past and for more moderately stable careers, such as nursing, medicine, dentistry, law and the military. In times of uncertainty, when our old institutions are breaking down and current high growth organisations operate in a state of perpetual flux; where paradigms are shifting, people are experiencing significant change and employers are having to revise their promises in attempts to achieve growth; the old adage 'what got you here, will no longer get you there' comes to the fore. We are living in a time of unprecedented change, transformational forces are in play and in an ever-changing world, the way in which you look at your career needs to radically change.

Be under no illusion, the world of work is undergoing transformation. We are witnessing several traditional industry sectors in decline and there are new areas of growth emerging. This is not a new phenomenon, it has been taking place for some time, for example there are jobs today that did not exist twelve years ago such as: social media strategists, app designer, Cloud computing technician, Millennial generational expert (generational consultants who help companies better understand the changing workforce), bloggers, online advertisers, green funeral directors and Sustainability specialists. You don't have to take my word for it, take a look at a study carried out by researchers at LinkedIn, one of the most popular networking sites for professionals. Carrying out a study of its extensive membership of over 225 million members, across 200 countries and territories around the world, researchers identified where there was growth and decline in today's economy by tracking people's jobs and job changes over a four-year period between 2007 and 2011. The snapshot revealed the following:

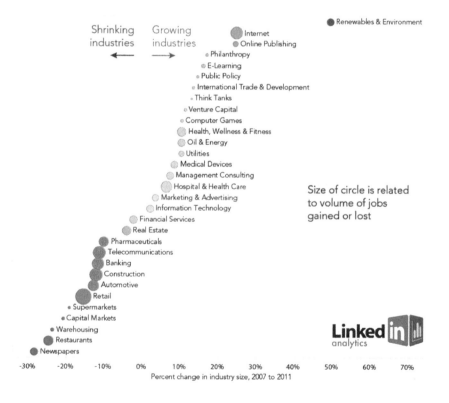

Admittedly one could argue that this research has an inherent bias; its members are highly motivated and technologically savvy, both of which are prerequisites for creating and maintaining a full profile on LinkedIn, which narrows the global workplace profile. However, the study acts as a good snapshot of career change during a period of global transformation, worldwide recession, where organisations are restructuring and downsizing and therefore a time when people are increasingly likely to be on the move. The key message here is to note that the job market evolves and to ensure you remain aware of trends.

A case in point is the well-documented fact that the traditional newspaper industry is in decline, advertising revenues are down and people are buying far less newspapers than they did in previous years. Interestingly, it is not that people are not interested in news; it is more about how people want to receive their news. Online news publications accessible on multimedia platforms are on the increase. If you were thinking of developing a career in journalism given this trend it would be folly to limit yourself to thinking solely about print media. You would need to think about online journalism and its associated skills to be employable in this sector in the future. A further transformational workplace change is that competition for jobs is no longer restricted to where you geographically live. With collaborative technology and partnering as standard, it is now commonplace for organisations to outsource, hire contractors, consultants and specialists from around the globe to fulfill their needs.

It saddens me to report that the pace of change, which has been swift, has meant a large percentage of educational and academic establishments are educating and training people today for many jobs that will not exist in the not-too-distant future. In reality they need to be developing and equipping people with the skills and knowledge for jobs that as yet do not exist. To stay employed in the future you will need to adjust your thinking and recognise the following: firstly, no organisation is going to guarantee you a lifetime career. The notion of a job for life is as obsolete as the typewriter. Secondly, you are going to need to create an adaptive career management strategy supported by regular updating of your knowledge and skills. Thirdly, as well as points one and two you will need to maintain an awareness of what is trending in the workplace or else you will find yourself forever playing catch-up or not being the first person of choice for new opportunities.

So how do you ensure you stay ahead of the career curve, remain nimble, agile and ensure you don't fall into career decline? In this action-orientated, how-to book, I will discuss with you why things have to change and what you need to do. This book is about helping you to build on your existing career and design a career management success strategy in order to survive and thrive in the future. You are provided with a simple but effective step-by-step guide to ensure that you have a career that meets your aspirations and affords you greater freedom and flexibility on how you work. Following the strategies presented, will enable you to seek out new opportunities, increase your earning potential based on your contribution as well as generate a high demand for your skills in your chosen area of expertise. You will find that the book works on several levels. You can simply read and digest the information and use it as a personal checklist to maintain your existing career path. Alternatively, if you engage fully and interact with the practical development activities presented, you get to dive deeply into the success philosophy that has worked effectively for many of my clients over the past fifteen years and continues to generate career success today. Undertake the journey and you will move from simple information acquisition and cross the mental – and possibly emotional – bridge to taking career-inspired action to thrive and achieve significant success in an environment of ongoing change.

Here is what you will explore

Each section in this book is designed around a career success principle and has some theory for the theorists, practical application for the pragmatists, reflection points for the reflectors and oodles of experiential activity for the activists. To get what you most need, scan the sections you find a little heavy and dive more deeply into the areas that resonate. In short, take what you need to create your career success strategy map.

Principle 1 – The Art of Mindfulness
This principle explores the kinds of work-related skills, abilities, behaviours and thinking, which will be in demand in the future. Looking at the research of futurologists you will be encouraged to think about what you need to do to ensure that you adapt and evolve, to ensure you have the skills and knowledge for the workplace of tomorrow.

Principle 2 – Know Thyself
Know thyself moves you beyond the traditional activities found in the career management space as it assumes you know your experience, skills and qualifications. It seeks to get you to identify the unconscious knowledge you hold about yourself and to gain clarity on your core attributes through the exploration of your multiple identities.

Principle 3 – Always Go North
This principle supports you in getting very clear about what you want and the reasons why you want what you do. In this section you will create a magnetic North Star that will begin to pull you unconsciously towards the future you've mapped out for yourself.

Principle 4: Step On The Path
Career success by design occurs when you know who you are,

where you come from, where you are now and where you are going. This principle focuses on cartography, the ability to design a unique and personalised career success map and to identify and overcome any obstacles in its path. Exploring key personal success components, you will learn how to take your route map from concept to practical reality, from internal thinking to external action.

Principle 5: Plug in to Action

As in computing, a plug-in is a component that adds specific capabilities to a generic application. Career success plug-ins contain essential additions to your career management plan to ensure your career development strategy is achieved.

The book closes with guidance on the creation of your career canvas and a career planning health warning. The latter is a mindfulness summary which reminds you of several of the key messages from your journey and encourages you to notice the effect you have on others as you increase your levels of success.

Icons and Tools

To get the most out of this book you may find it useful to create a career management strategy notebook, if you don't already have one. The notebook can act as a place where you can capture your thinking and ideas as you complete the various activities presented. In addition it is a place to craft, create and hold your final career strategy map.

To help you navigate the text you will notice a range of icons that encourage you to pause, reflect, undertake an activity or to take action. These are as follows:

The leaf exists to remind you to pause, pay close attention or to take note of a key point of information.

◎   The target acts a pause for reflection and to raise the questions you need to ask yourself.

⧗   The hourglass symbol is a summary of key messages and acts as an aide-memoire for you to use in the future.

Ⓐ This is an activity symbol and lets you know that you are going to be asked to undertake a development activity.

With the exception of Principle 3, at the end of each section you will find a page titled **Take Action Now**. It invites you to answer questions or summarise your learning and chunk it into something meaningful that will contribute towards the creation of your success map.

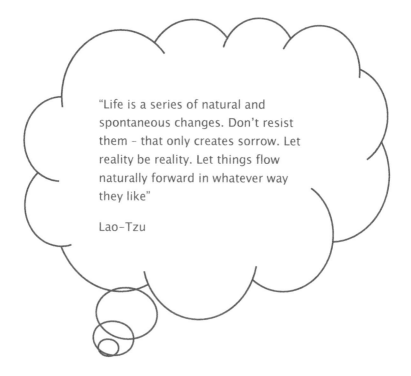

"Life is a series of natural and spontaneous changes. Don't resist them – that only creates sorrow. Let reality be reality. Let things flow naturally forward in whatever way they like"

Lao-Tzu

PRINCIPLE

The Art of Mindfulness

One of the fundamentals to your future career success lies in you becoming more mindful. This is the ability to be consciously observant of the trends that are up-and-coming and paying attention to emerging patterns of change particularly in the workplace. By cultivating this ability you will naturally develop greater career agility and flexibility, enabling you to gain first-mover advantage should you desire, as opposed to being the person that follows reluctantly behind the herd or arrives late and finds that others have beaten them to the rewards.

Fortunately for the mindful few, futurologists, forecasters and researchers have made identifying and accessing demographic and big shift trend information easier for all of us. Just by allocating a small amount of Internet exploration time you will find this data readily available for every aspect of your life. At the time of writing, forecasting studies reveal there are a number of big disruptive shifts that will likely reshape the future landscape of work in the next ten years. Summarised here are four of the megatrends that will have a significant impact on the workplace going forward and an outline of several core skills, which will be essential for future career success.

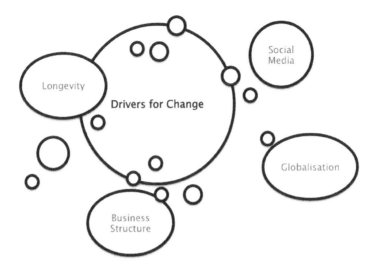

Megatrend 1: We are living longer

The continuous reduction in adult mortality combined with lower fertility rates means the populations of many countries of the world are rapidly ageing. "Population ageing is unprecedented, without parallel in the history of humanity. Increases in the proportions of older persons (60 years or older) are being accompanied by declines in the proportions of the young (under age 15). By 2050, the number of older persons in the world will exceed the number of young for the first time in history." (United Nations, 2001)[1] Over the last thirty years the number of centenarians, people aged one hundred years or more, in the UK has increased five fold from 2,500 in 1980 to 12,640 in 2010. (ONS, 2012)[2]. In the US it is estimated that by 2025, the number of Americans over the age of sixty will increase by 70%.

This unprecedented demographic change is already having a profound and transformational impact on many societies. Population ageing, where older people account for a proportionally larger share of the total population, has a direct impact on a broad range of economic, political and social processes, and this directly affects you. As people live longer, benefits, such as pensions, healthcare or old-age support, need to be paid over longer periods. Older people will increasingly demand products and services to support more healthy and active senior years. New perceptions of what it means to 'age' will begin to emerge.

As a result you will need to reassess your approach to your career, family life, and education to accommodate this demographic shift. Already in Europe retirement ages are being redrawn and people are expected to work past the age of sixty-five. Multiple careers will become commonplace and lifelong learning will be the norm with preparation for occupational change initiatives becoming an area of major growth. Organisations will need to restructure human resource and talent management strategies and if you haven't already, you will have to rethink the notion of a traditional career path.

Megatrend 2: Rapid technological change.

According to research from the Institute for the Future (2011) an independent, non-profit strategic research group with more than forty years of forecasting experience in identifying emerging trends and discontinuities that will transform global society and the global marketplace: "We are on the cusp of a major transformation in our relationships with our tools – the apparatus we need to live our daily lives and conduct our work. Over the next decade, new smart machines will enter offices, factories, and homes in numbers never seen before". We are already seeing and experiencing how new multimedia technologies are bringing about a transformation in the way in which we share information, and communicate with family, friends, colleagues, customers and suppliers. This field will continue to evolve with emergent technologies such as digital animation, augmented reality and robotics coming to the fore and becoming more widespread. We will begin to develop new expectations, require new tools, use new jargon and begin to further evolve the way in which we use new media to exchange information and communicate. We are already witnessing the demise of text-based communication on the Internet as it migrates to more visual communication media, which includes video and animation. Have you noticed when you put an item into a search engine that video-based listings are appearing early in your search listings? This trend will become more evident in the workplace with communication becoming more evolutionary and transitory.

At the same time there is a growth in the use of virtual networks such as Facebook, Twitter and YouTube which now form a core part of many people's daily lives. The millions of users generating and viewing multimedia content from their smartphones, tablets and laptops are creating significant cultural and communication shifts. New media with its ability to enable new ways for groups to come together and collaborate is bringing about new levels of transparency that will have an impact on how we deliver our work. The rules of today will not be the rules of tomorrow, as the boundaries between work and personal networks will continue to merge. Individuals will tap into the resources embedded in their social connections to access collective intelligence, to problem solve as well as share experiences.

Megatrend 3: Business Structures

Many of the educational and corporate structures we see today have been built around old social norms. However as profound societal and technological change takes place, a new generation of organisational development structures, concepts and skill requirements will emerge. If an enterprise is not prepared or flexible enough to be able to adjust its products, services or internal processes at a quick pace, it risks losing ground to the international competitors who are. The retail sector is proof of adaptivity in response to change, being quick to respond to changing purchasing patterns. For example, large retailers diversified their offering combining the high street retail experience with online technology as their customers began voting with their feet to online shopping. Personal banking evolved its structures in response to change as it moved from offering just a branch service through to telephone banking and now most banks deliver a full suite of online and mobile services. An individual never has to meet a bank staff member face to face if they no longer wish.

Business to consumer operations that keep pace with customers' demands and use emergent technology, naturally evolve. This trend is creating a rethink about business structures, staff development and utilisation. In the future businesses will create structures that go beyond the way they transact business today. As innovation takes place, future workplace thinking is being shaped not by traditional management/organisational theory but from fields such as game design, neuroscience, and the field of happiness psychology. Greater use of social media tools, flexible-working contracts, blended-learning solutions, collaborative partnerships with suppliers and former competitors will drive the creation of the businesses of the future.

Megatrend 4: Globalisation

Globalisation is the removal of boundaries and the effective integration of communication and delivery of products, services and business across different geographic borders. For example, a sportswear manufacturer can design its products in Europe, make them in South East Asia and sell them in North America. The world is now globally connected and very inter-dependent. In a truly globally connected world, cultural diversity will become a greater source of innovation. A worker's skill set could see them working not only within diverse cultural groups in a virtual setting. They could quite feasibly be posted to any number of geographical locations, as organisations seek to maintain their competitive edge, maintain international levels of market share and/or break into new markets.

So what?

What is the significance of these megatrends for career planning? With these megatrends impacting our future what does this mean for the skills deemed necessary to thrive in the workplace? To underestimate the disruptive impact of these trends presented is naïve at best, they will have and are already having a profound impact. These trends are informing the skills and competency requirements that employers are seeking in the future. So significant are these emergent trends that a myriad of studies have been commissioned by national governments across the world. They are notably concerned about future economic growth, business competitiveness, workforce development skills and future employability. In response to emergent trends, these studies identify how these current megatrends present challenges to companies and are reflected in the skill and knowledge requirements needed for the future at different levels of an organisation. In a study carried out by the European Centre for the Development of Vocational Training (Cedefop)[3], on the challenges and trends in the continuing development of skills and career development of the European workforce (2012), they found that large companies within the European Union who were known for their innovative and sophisticated human resource development practices, were generally satisfied with identifying and sourcing the delivery of professional and technical skills. However, the picture was far from the same when it came to identifying and ensuring that their staff have transversal skills. These are the skills that are not specifically related to one's occupation, but are important and relevant to the successful delivery of work and the future success of a company.

🍃 In addition to the megatrends described, there are five core future skills as well as your area of expertise that will be essential for you in the future.

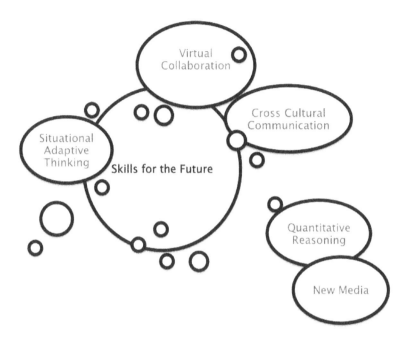

Future Skill 1: Situational Adaptive Thinking

Situational Adaptive Thinking is the ability to think and come up with solutions and responses beyond existing frames of reference and constraints in the present moment. Research by MIT professor and economist, David Autor[4], presents evidence that in 'industrialised economies the structure of job opportunities and employment growth is "polarizing" into relatively high skill, high wage jobs and low skill, low wage jobs.' His research goes on to demonstrate that there is a narrowing and contracting number of opportunities in middle wage and middle skill white and blue collar jobs. The key contributor to this job polarisation is the automation of routine work and the outsourcing of 'routine' tasks to international labour markets. Routine tasks, as described by economists David Autor, Frank Levy, and Richard Murnane, are job activities that are sufficiently well defined that they can be carried out successfully by either a computer executing a program or by a comparatively less well-educated and/or lower-paid worker in a developing country. The high skill and low skill categories where there is high employment growth both require what Autor terms as 'situational adaptability'. This is the ability to respond to unique and unexpected circumstances in the moment. Futurologists inform us that the skill of situational adaptability will be at a premium in the next decade, particularly as automation and outsourcing is set to continue. It will require you to be able to think innovatively and quickly adapt your reasoning in the face of new information and/or questioning.

◉How situational adaptive are you? Are you currently in a role that a computer programme could fulfil in the not-too-distant future?

Future Skill 2: Cross Cultural Communication

Cross cultural communication is simply the ability to operate in different cultural settings. Increasing globalisation increases the importance of staff possessing high levels of cross cultural communication competencies and relevant language skills. This will become an important skill for all workers, not just those who have to operate in diverse geographical environments. Companies seeking growth in new and emerging markets recognise that just having English-speaking staff is no longer sufficient. In countries such as China and Russia it is difficult to enter the market if you do not know the language or the cultural norms and nuances. As organisations become truly globally connected and as their staff increasingly migrate from different geographical areas for work, or collaborate in virtual teams across cultural boundaries, they increasingly perceive diversity as a driver for business success. Diversity is no longer being perceived as just a moral or employment legislation compliance issue. The long-term research is now demonstrating that the ability to transcend difference, build effective relationships, and work and communicate effectively as part of a diverse team is fast becoming a core workplace competency and key ingredient to business financial success[5].

◉How many different nationalities or different cultures do you interact with in a typical day? What do you know about the cultural norms of cultures other than your own?

Future Skill 3: Quantitative Reasoning

Quantitative Reasoning is the ability to translate large amounts of data into abstract concepts and to understand data-based reasoning. We live and work in an environment that is brimming with information; the amount of data that we have at our disposal is vast and will continue to increase. The consequence is that many more roles in the workplace will require individuals to be able to read and analyse data, create relevant models or scenarios, draw inferences, make recommendations and take appropriate action. In the absence of credible data, staff will be expected to make decisions and take appropriate action. The by-product of processing large amounts of information from multiple devices and accessing a diverse range of information streams is that it may lead to information fatigue or cognitive overload. In the future, organisations and their staff will need to learn to effectively filter and focus on that which is deemed to be important and develop techniques and strategies for tackling the problem of cognitive overload.

9

Future Skill 4: New Media Literacy

New media literacy is the ability to use new media platforms and to be able to leverage these for effective communication. You will not be considered literate in this century unless you become well versed in all the media that are used to communicate effectively in the workplace. In the next ten years, communication tools that break away from the heavily text-based, multi-deck PowerPoint slide approach will become the standard. The next generation of workers will need to become fluent in a range of visual information communication forms and tools such as video and digital animation. The ability to create visually stimulating presentations as well as to follow the flow of stories, conversation and information across multiple modalities will become the norm to engage and influence audiences, as will the ability to critically assess information in this format.

Future Skill 5: Virtual Collaboration

Virtual collaboration is the ability to work productively as a member of a virtual team. With the advent of connective technologies the co-location of staff, advisers and consultants is no longer essential. Virtual team working is no longer in its infancy and is the fact of life for many in large corporations. New working competencies and protocols continue to emerge in order to make this working style productive as leaders and their teams adjust to this different style of working. These include: the creation of virtual shared environments that develop interpersonal relationships and build trust, and the recreation of social and emotional interactions that foster the benefits of team working typically experienced when people are co-located for extended periods of time.

Every two years for the last decade, IBM has sat down with CEOs and public sector leaders in every part of the world to gauge their perspective on emerging trends and issues. The 2012 IBM CEO Study[6] identified and analyzed trends through the eyes of more than 1,700 CEOs and public sector leaders. They found that across industries and geographies, CEOs consistently highlighted four personal characteristics most critical for employees' future success: 1. Being collaborative, 2. Being communicative, 3. Being creative and 4. Flexibility. These qualities were seen as being fundamental if employees were going to thrive in the organisations these CEOs were creating.

Take Note

As we depart from our exploration of this principle, hopefully you now have a better appreciation of the important need for mindfulness – the art of being consciously observant. The constant transformational change in both product and service demands, regulatory frameworks, socio-demographics and the rapid pace of technological advancement will not disappear. Recognition of the shifting organisational landscape is an essential key to your future career success, as is the understanding of the kinds of work skills, abilities, behaviours and thinking that will be in demand in the future. Principle 1 teaches that the successful individuals of tomorrow will be those who continuously up-skill, adapt and evolve.

Take Action Now

Here are two simple actions that you can do to help you create your career management success strategy.

1. Take note of what's trending for you.

2. Reflecting on future trends, identify two future skills that you know you will need to develop.

Moving On

Temporarily park these answers or reflections, as you will have an opportunity to revisit them later. It is time to gain clarity on your unique demonstrable talents and gifts.

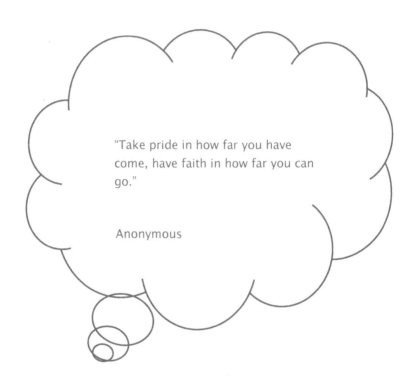

"Take pride in how far you have come, have faith in how far you can go."

Anonymous

PRINCIPLE

Know Thyself

'Gnothi seauton' is the famous Greek maxim meaning 'Know Thyself'. For centuries, people seeking advice from the oracle at Delphi would read this inscription and be inspired. Throughout the years philosophers such as Socrates offered this same advice to their students as a means of encouragement on how to gain insights and knowledge. By looking in the mirror of self-awareness you learn not just about yourself, but also about your relationships, motivations, ambition and your areas of bias. It is this underlying principle – know thyself, which we turn to in planning the next phase of your career. I am not referring to the typical carrying out of a personal skills audit or a personal SWOT analysis; you should know this stuff already. In truth what got you to this point in your career, as we can see from the drivers for change and future skills, is not what is going to get you to where you want to go in the future. Equally I'm not suggesting any heavy-duty soul-searching either as it's widely accepted that there will always be some things people are not very good at knowing about themselves. We never have a complete view on how we are perceived by others because we do not 'stand in their shoes' i.e. see the world through the filter of their lives or experiences. However, there are some things you do know about yourself beyond a doubt and it is these you need to capture.

Although I do not know you personally I can confidently say that in your career going forward you will want to ensure you are doing more of what you enjoy and what makes you feel good, rather than that which saps your energy and demotivates you. I support the view of Raymond Aaron, a *New York Times* top ten best selling author and success coach, when he talks about setting work and financial goals. He states that ideally your goal should be to be able to say: "I love this so much, it is the *only* thing I will do for money". Now, that's a fulfilling aspiration and something to strive for. Pause for a few seconds; imagine for a moment that you are in a role that you enjoy so much that you'd never contemplate doing anything else for money. If the doubter-critic voice in your head is now whispering to you that such things can never happen or that thinking like this is not for mere mortals such as you, then you have a little work to do on your autopilot thinking.

In a short while I'm going to invite you to undertake a couple of know thyself-development activities. The challenge is that you won't do them, perhaps telling yourself you'll come back to it later, or you may start them and over intellectualise the process which will only reveal responses that you want to hear and that will keep you safe in the status quo of your life. Remember you've picked up this book to get answers and these activities are designed to work and are proven to achieve results.

Your brain has an enormous capacity to store and process information as well as the ability to control all human activity. As a consequence it needs to find efficient ways to store and access its information quickly. The way you think about events, challenges and problems is not haphazard: there is a pattern to it and that pattern is psychologically efficient and very habitual. Human beings are very much creatures of habit, we think and behave along the lines of what has been described as the raindrop principle (Ryde, R 2007)[7]. When you give thought to how to tackle a problem or a challenge you act very much on autopilot. This has been likened to a raindrop winding its way down a windowpane. You would perhaps think that a raindrop landing on the window could take a multitude of routes down the pane of glass, however that is not the case. There are two important factors in play: the first is gravity, which puts pressure on the raindrop to take the most direct route, and the second is the path already taken by previous raindrops, which act as channels encouraging subsequent raindrops to follow the same journey.

Human neuroscience studies show us that our direction of thinking and therefore behaving is very much the same, that is it follows direct routes and existing pathways. Through studying the chemical and electrical changes that occur in the brain neuroscientists have demonstrated that there is a direct connection between the mind and body. We are hardwired to store information and experiences for later retrieval in the form of easily accessible automatic responses. To make experiences stick we create memories, which we repeatedly think about.

Ever found yourself preoccupied by an event or experience and run it over and over in your mind? Ever found yourself persistently musing about something that recently happened? When this set of actions is occurring in your mind, you are creating and strengthening neural pathways. The pathways are networks or collections of neurons that work together. A neuron is simply a nerve cell in the brain. The human brain is made up of approximately 100 billion (100,000,000,000) neurons, which represents a lot of processing and storage power. Repetitive thoughts are neural pathway reinforcers and are an essential process in making thoughts and events quickly accessible for future use.

Have you also noticed that when you are musing, reflecting or reliving an experience that other thoughts and feelings also pop into your mind? They may be similar experiences that happened to you or perhaps events you observed elsewhere. These associations are not random; they are what is called associated memory. These associations ensure that the new neuron builds a long-term relationship with these other memories. What has occurred is the building of a neural network that is 'wired' together. When any one of these past experiences is triggered they all 'fire' together. This enables you to quickly access critical information drawing from past thinking or experience in order to make speedy decisions.

This process of memory and learning has been attributed to Dr Hebb (1970)[8] and is often referred to as the 'fire together, wire together principle.' It explains how we incorporate new knowledge and experiences into our brains. For example imagine you want to learn to ride a motorbike. You can already drive a car and as a child you learnt to ride a bike. Because of these experiences you already have clusters of neurons that wired together when learning these skills, such as being able to balance and knowing which way to lean when turning a corner on a bike. You know which side of the road to drive on, and have an awareness of signaling and mirror usage from learning to drive a car. When you start to ride a motorbike the pre-wired neurons start to fire, you remember everything. As a consequence although operating the motorbike will require some new learning it will be easier than mastering it had you never ridden a bike or driven a car as the experiences are mostly familiar.

We have a range of habitual thinking and behaviour patterns drawn from our experiences that behave almost like the gravitational force on the raindrop running down the windowpane. Repetitive actions lead us to create our own channels (habits) in which we can become stuck. Neural networks fire together more strongly the more they are activated together. Continuous neural activation is what creates behavioural habits and thinking styles.

Have you ever travelled from home to work, taking the same route that you take virtually every day and wondered how you got there? When I worked in the field of psychological trauma one of the challenges for emergency services staff in attempting to rescue or evacuate passengers was that despite an exit being blocked, people still wanted to leave the scene by their 'usual' route. The gravitational pull of these unseen channels of habit is strong. Continuous neural activation linked with emotion i.e. how we feel about the wired experiences is what creates habitual or automatic thinking and behaviour. If the experience feels positive we are more likely to want to seek a repetition of the feeling.

So what has this got to do with career planning and knowing yourself? The answer is simple – everything! If you are feeling stuck in your career, uncertain about what steps or which direction to take next; if you are a victim of autopilot thinking and feel as if you are in a rut; these next series of activities will be beneficial as they encourage you to switch this thinking off, to take notice of your patterns, be focused and creative and to identify key ingredients for your career going forward.

Creating your best job yet.

If you need some clarity and assistance on identifying what your best job going forward would be, these next activity steps will help you design your best job yet. If you are very clear on what that is you may want to skip this next section.

Step 1 Firstly, you need to gather a pile of scrap paper or post-it notes and a pen or pencil. You are going to generate an unedited and uncensored list of your loves. Note I have said loves not shoulds, maybes or aspirations. These loves are real and focus on your career to date.

18

(A) I want you to think about all the jobs you have done so far and throw noodles at the wall and see what sticks. By this I mean imagine you can have as many 'noodles' as you wish, each noodle is something that you love about the jobs you've had thus far. Write one item per sheet of paper or post-it note. Scrunch it into a ball and throw it at a wall or into an empty bowl or basket. This needs to be done very quickly and with some energy. Write an item and throw it. Don't worry about repeats just keep scribbling. Repeat the activity until you have all your loves in a pile. It is important you do not over-think or judge your responses, just jot down what comes to mind. If writing poses you a challenge or paper is scarce then find someone who knows you well, perhaps a friend or family member, and ask them to yell quickly at you: "What do you love?" Then you yell back as fast as you can, without thinking, one thing you love about your previous jobs to date. Your friend then yells back: "What do you love?" Again, you reply. Keep this up until you slow down or run out of new loves, which will likely be after about twelve to sixteen answers. Your friend must adopt a rapid-fire approach to asking you the question not allowing long pauses.

◎ Once you have completed the activity notice how you are feeling, what is the voice in your head saying? There are useful reflective insights to be gained from how you approached the task. Just pause for a few seconds and make a mental note: did you follow instruction and do it immediately; choose the friend approach, if so why? Did you tweak the process or just dive in? Perhaps you scheduled time and took time to carefully prepare? Whatever your approach it will tell you something about yourself and the way you prefer to tackle new tasks in general. What is it?

Step 2   Now you've got a list of loves you need to analyse them and see which ones stick. The question to you is this: in the next stage of your career which of these loves do you definitely want to keep and most importantly, why? How you complete this next stage of the exercise is up to you, however typically what works is this. Take a blank sheet of paper any size that you prefer – A4, A3 or flipchart if you like the big stuff. Pick up some pens and take a reflective look at all your 'noodles' and decide which you definitely want in the next stage of your career. Create your love list down one side of the paper. Do not be surprised if other items pop into your head, these can be added too. Remember it's just your neurons firing and wiring together. You can have as many or as little as you like on your love list. Once completed next to each item write a brief comment to yourself as to why this item is important. Be honest with yourself. If you are struggling as to why it is important then perhaps it's a 'should' item and doesn't belong on this list.

Step 3   Once you have a list of your loves and have identified why they are important to you, your next task is to rate their level of importance. Simply go down the list and mark each item as being of high importance or low importance to you.

Step 4   Having identified the levels of importance of your loves, carefully identify up to three loves of high importance that you would keep if you were creating a job that you loved so much and it was the *only* thing you would do for money. An example of a love list:

Love List	Why Important	High/Low Importance	Absolute Must
Big international projects	Great people to work with, used all my skills, I was doing something that mattered and makes a difference.	High	✔
Pay and bonuses	Rewarded properly for my worth, which meant I was able to have great holidays, buy what I wanted without having to worry about money too much.	High	
Status	People listened to what I had to say. Felt important.	High	✔
Great offices	Didn't have to commute for too long. The office had character and I didn't have to hot desk.	Low	

This love list is a snapshot of what is really important to you now in this phase of your life and career. Be aware, if your personal circumstances change then so will steps 3 and 4. However if you have been honest with yourself and your life is not scheduled to change imminently you now have insight into several important items that you can add to your career success strategy, which you will be compiling later. You also have a very important component of an activity you will undertake in the next principle.

What do you bring to the party?

At the time of writing there is no doubt that it is currently an employers' market when we look at the current recruitment space. Economically we are in a protracted global recession. The impact of the economic crisis was unprecedented in terms of speed, magnitude and geographic scope. As a result organisations across the globe have been restructuring, merging, downsizing or seeking to make efficiency savings. The outcome of which is that the need for retaining and attracting good people has never been more important. The strategic consequence of this kind of organisational change is that there emerges a large pool of experienced candidates sitting in jobs feeling vulnerable, thinking about moving but scared to take the risk, those sitting, dreaming of being headhunted and those being released into the job market due to redundancy. Combine this with a large number of graduates coming out of colleges and universities unable to find work. The result is that at all levels of recruitment this allows employers to be very picky. As companies receive hundreds of CVs for each job opening that they advertise, they are seeking candidates that can fulfill a more diverse range of criteria beyond just expertise and past experience. Imagine you're at an interview and you are asked a perfectly reasonable question: "Why should I hire you?" To which you may reply something akin to:

"As you can see from my application, I am highly experienced and highly qualified for the role. I have high levels of integrity, am loyal, hardworking, and dependable, as well as being a good team player..."

If the interviewer is lucky you might even give an example or two of the evidence that supports this statement. Now put yourself in the interviewer's seat for a moment and imagine you have just received this response from candidate number nine. Most of the candidates that preceded this one had said something similar! Can you imagine how uninspiring a response like this can be perceived and how very little answers like this showcase a candidate positively or provide enough information to differentiate one candidate from another? Interview questions which ask "why should I give you the job", are a gift, at any level of seniority, if you know yourself and know what you want. They represent an ideal opportunity for you to really market yourself to the interviewer, your opportunity to wow and differentiate yourself from the competition. Drawing from your wealth of experience, expertise, personal style and your aspirations you have an opportunity to present your uniqueness as a solution to the problem faced by the prospective employer i.e. finding the right person to fill an important post. This next suggested activity will help you understand how you see yourself and how others perceive you. Each of us has multiple identities and persona, which we adopt in differing situations and often vary dependent upon who we are with. These multiple identities can reveal much about who we really are as well as identify key skills and act as a catalyst for uncovering your motivations and aspirations.

(A) **Suggested activity:** Taking a blank sheet of paper or fresh page in your notebook, carry out the following steps to create a comprehensive profile of yourself through the lens of your relationship with others.

Step 5   Identify all the different roles or identities that you currently fulfil. Include both personal and professional.

Step 6   Draw a circle and divide it into segments. In each segment write a role or identity. Create as many segments as you can. See the examples provided.

Personal:

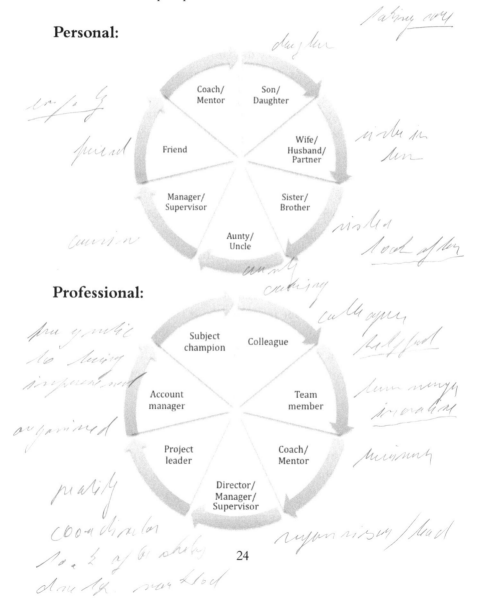

Professional:

24

Step 7   Next to each section, create a list of words or short phrases that answers the question: What is it that I do that makes me a great... *insert segment item*? For example: What is it that makes me a great team member? Please be focused here, when we introspect about what we're thinking or feeling, we can often get it wrong in our subconscious desire to feel good. The importance in this exercise is to try to be as honest, purposeful and objective as you can. This is an exercise in identifying what you do and making a judgment about whether you do it really well.

Step 8   Having completed this profile take a close look at what you have written. Highlight the words or phrases that are repeated or that particularly resonate with you. Ask yourself if there are any patterns or trends that have emerged? Notice what stories or associated memories bubbled up when you were creating the profile and trawl these for insights about yourself. Here is a work profile example:

What is it that I do that makes me a great...

I'm a patient teacher. I always **find solutions** to colleague **difficulties**

I'm **helpful** to my colleagues and I do my job well and thus **contribute to the team** bonus pot.

I listen to client needs, understand their business and anticipate their problems. Match client needs to our service offering.

I make myself **available to answer questions** and to show them the ropes. Long **after the buddy system is over.**

IT trouble shooter

Team member

Key Account Manager

New starter Mentor

Project leader

I go the **extra mile** and really **add value.**

I always **exceed my sales targets.**

I am a master planner and organiser.

I consistently **deliver** against targets and on time.

Key Words/Phrases/Message:

Helpful, Listen and understand what is required,

Problem solver, Always over deliver, Make money

Imagine you are back at the interview and have been asked the 'why should we hire you' question. A response built on your evidenced key words and phrases will differentiate you from the others that have gone before. Using the example above a response could be: "I consistently over deliver against set targets, whilst adding real value to clients and team colleagues. I achieve this because I take time to understand needs and design innovative cost-effective solutions to their challenges and problems."

The more focused you can make your profile wheels the better able you are to look at yourself, as if in a mirror. In live programmes participants are often surprised at what this activity reveals. Having completed the eight activity steps it is time to pull everything together you've completed so far to support the creation of your success formula. Note this is not your final plan; it is designed to help you get clear and give you a sense check. Is this who I am and what I want to take forward?

1. Utilising your love list create a simple statement which identifies what you want to maintain or take forward into your ideal job in the future.

    Please write this in the present tense, as you are creating a new neural pathway and rewiring relevant past experiences to support it. An example statement may look like this: *In my ideal job I am working on a large international project, which makes a difference to the lives of others. I am utilising all my skills and expertise, whilst working with a group of great like-minded and ambitious professional people.*

2. Now add to your statement a few lines about what you bring to the party. (What are you great at?) For example: *I'm*

recognised for my ability to communicate, take decisive action, make level-headed decisions, stay calm under pressure and generate new ideas when people get stuck.

3. Carry out a sense check, I want you to read what you have written in the above points as a whole statement and see how it fits. Does it feel right or is it out of kilter with who you are? Does it feel superficial or does it have profound depth? Do you want to take this aspect of yourself forward or are there some things you wish to change? Pay attention to your thoughts and feelings. Change what you wish to ensure you are comfortable; however do make sure it is based on your knowledge of who you are.

⌛ If you are happy with what you have stated it's time to move on. If not, pause and quickly revisit the activities and your answers and tease out anything that you may have missed.

Take Note

Gaining knowledge of the self is not a simple or quick task if undertaken thoroughly. Even when the benefits are obvious it is often something that people tend to resist or once they have embarked on the journey stay superficial, lie to themselves or quit too soon. Making time to take an honest look at yourself provides you with the opportunity to compare the self you want to be with the person you are presenting to the world. However, reflection on its own or for reflection's sake will achieve nothing. It is what you do with the knowledge you gain from the exercise that will deliver the rewards. Principle 2 teaches that knowledge of the self affords you the opportunity to create the person you want to be and craft the future you desire.

Take Action Now

Nothing in life changes until *we* change. In order to remain an attractive talent in your industry space and in response to the future skill demands and trends outlined in Principle 1, what do you need to do or consider?

Moving On

You know who you are and have gained an idea of several skills you need to develop going forward. Now it's time to build a magnetic vision for the future.

"Where your talents and the needs of the world cross, therein lies your calling."

Aristotle

PRINCIPLE 3

Always Go North

In 1998 Daniel Goleman stated "Except for the financially desperate, people do not work for money alone. What also fuels their passion for work is a larger sense of purpose or passion. Given the opportunity, people gravitate to what gives them meaning, to what engages to the fullest their commitment, talent, energy and skill." If Goleman and many of his contemporaries are correct, then this chapter may be the most important for you in designing your career management success strategy.

For many years, the North Star has been used as a navigational aid by explorers and travellers. The North Star would act as both a guide and as a measurement on how far they had journeyed. If ever they found they were uncertain of which direction to take, or there were no other landmarks by which to navigate, they would look heavenwards for the North Star. This star is the brightest and fixed star, which can always be found and used without error to signpost the right direction. This idea of a guiding star can be found in many different religious and cultural traditions and it can act as a strong metaphor for us all. Every goal that you set and aspiration, or ambition that you desire, brings with it the risks of distraction and derailment. However, if you have identified your North Star, when you find yourself in those moments of doubt, confusion or overwhelm, if you steadfastly hold your North Star to your mind you will feel its pull. It will keep you orientated and act as a powerful magnet that will naturally and automatically keep you moving forward. When planning your career in changing times, when you can no longer predict or plan your way to success as you did before, the identification of your career North Star can be immensely useful as north is the only direction worth moving towards to achieve your dreams and aspirations.

An effective way to create your career North Star is to build an archetype of what you really want. A career archetype is a composite representation, a prototype model that describes the set of core components of what you desire. The more comprehensive and tangible you can design it the stronger the magnetic effect and the less likely you are to give it up at the whim of an external influence. It will motivate and inspire you through the natural highs and lows of organisational change, periods of transition and even job loss. It will quietly drive your levels of motivation and move you towards your future success. What is great is that it is easy to do.

Step 1   **Dreamcatcher**
In this activity you are going to partake in some creative daydreaming. So it is important that you find approximately ten minutes when you know you will not be interrupted. In the past daydreaming had a poor reputation and was never really given serious consideration. Today as studies into the mind and how it functions have become prevalent, neuroscience research is showing that productive daydreaming, or positive visioning as it is referred to in business, aids working memory, supports creativity and can act as a protective mechanism in times of frustration and stress. For this creative process to be effective you will need space and time to allow your mind to wander. You will need to be able to notice your mind wandering and to catch the ideas when you have them. This is an active, creative process – what good would it have done Albert Einstein, a big fan of the daydream, if he hadn't noticed his ideas?

Before you begin your creative daydream I want you to undertake a warm-up exercise. Start by getting yourself into a relatively balanced mental state. For example go and use the bathroom or have a drink of water. Get as relaxed as you can and then simply spend a few minutes thinking about someone who you professionally admire. Gently explore and notice what it is that you admire about them. Don't worry if you only notice one or two things; this is just a warm-up designed to settle your mind and prepare you for the main activity.

Ⓐ Now that you have successfully got into the creative daydream space you can start your daydream for real. After reading this next paragraph close your eyes and imagine: it is three years from now and you are sat in a café having a coffee or tea with a really good friend who you haven't seen in a while. You've been catching up on news, laughing, joking and remembering and you've just started sharing a detailed story about the great job you are currently doing. Imagine yourself having this conversation, look around notice the surroundings, the smells and the noise and hubbub around you both. As you begin talking, listen carefully to what you are saying to this good friend about the really great job that you are currently in. Close your eyes now and imagine the scene described.

◎ If you are struggling to get started take a few deep breaths and remember you already have some components of this story from the *throwing noodles at the wall*, *knowing what you bring to the party* and *future skills and trends* activities. Begin by describing these. Please note this activity comes with a little warning – don't consciously daydream when you are supposed to be concentrating on doing something else, such as operating complex machinery, working with a heat source, driving a car or motorcycle or such like, that will be a recipe for disaster. Be sensible and be safe.

Step 2　**Capture the dream**

In simple notes quickly capture your daydream before it fades. Distil the components and jot down what you told your good friend about your amazing job. You may want to repeat the process over a few days and see what happens. Coaching clients who have undertaken this activity report that returning to the daydream between sessions provided greater clarity and technicolour to the conversation they were having with their friend. They began to imagine their friend asking interesting questions and found they were able to answer the questions fully. Several people added a conversation with the person they most professionally admired. Participants in this exercise often comment on how they began to see everything in minute detail. For some it ceased to be just a daydream and started to become reality. However clear your conversation was in your imaginative journey, the content of your conversation comprises the key components of where you want to take your career.

Step 3　**North Star**

The next step is to construct your North Star. This is achieved by identifying your career success archetype, a prototype model of the place to where you are going. With your mind now very clear about the components of what you want to achieve, you can have fun and be as creative or minimalist as you wish. Your next action is to create a very clear and comprehensive statement of your career success design i.e. a clear and comprehensive statement or vision of what you want which draws inspiration from the daydream as well as your current personal circumstances.

This is an important step; if you aim at nothing in life you will hit it every time. Highly successful people have a destination in mind, a goal or objective that they are seeking to achieve. They understand that you can't hit a target if you can't see it. Imagine a game of basketball without any basketball hoops, a game of hockey or football without a goal to aim for, a company without a strategic vision. There is always a clearly defined target, which is being aimed for. You need a vision or target for your career success and you now have all the ingredients to describe what you desire. In your design of this archetype don't feel constrained by pen and paper, you may prefer to use video – create a mini video of yourself talking to camera about this great job. If you love to write then produce a creative narrative story describing this great job. If you are familiar with the concept of the vision board, this is an ideal opportunity to generate an 'I know what I want' vision board. Set out to find images to portray your vision by tearing them from magazines, newspapers or photos. Once you have a collection you can then paste them as a collage on paper. The process is simple, but very powerful. It is always important when selecting images to eliminate any that do not feel right, your intuition will support you in the process if you pay attention. Lay out your vision board in a way that works for you, but I encourage you to put yourself in the centre, either using a photo or to write your name in big letters. Remember whichever mode you use to capture your career success archetype it is important that what you create must appeal to your deepest self. There is no template for this activity, it needs to be your personal design and whatever you create, be it a vision board to a few words, it must feel compelling to you. Where you find yourself making a general statement become clear about what it means to you. For example if you use the descriptor 'I love my job' be able to answer the question "what specifically is it that you love"? If you are working with a great team, what specifically is it about the team that makes it great. If you mentioned your working environment specify what it is that makes it great for you, such as sitting by a large window with an amazing view of a park. Have you an office rather than open plan working? Do you have a thirty-minute commute as opposed to the two hours that you have at the moment? Is there flexible working or you only work three days per week? Get into the colourful detail of what you want for yourself.

Try not to rush this activity, the more specificity you can assign the more compelling it will become. Do not worry if it feels currently unobtainable, that is OK. Remember that maybe your autopilot thinking and doubter critic internal voice are just doing their job of keeping you safe in the now. Creating pictures in your mind has an ability to make reality respond. It is the principle behind company strategic planning, creative design, works of art, and all product and service design.

Visualisation is not a new technique, it has been used by many successful individuals across diverse sectors. It is widely used in the high performance arena of business, sport, and the arts while health care professionals encourage its use in complex treatment modalities. In almost any aspect of life, be it career, home, or even sports, an important ingredient for success is positive visioning. However, the ability to move from dreams to reality does not happen on its own. As in the world of sport it occurs in conjunction with action and practise; together these two factors can yield very powerful results. We explore this more fully in the next principle. I also encourage you to pay attention to what language you are using to create your career success North Star. Are you writing it in the present tense or future? On video did you talk about it as if it were in three years time or have you said *I am…?* When describing your vision board have you described it to yourself or anyone else in the present or past tense? You are deliberately being asked to create a tension gap between your current career situation and where you want to be. If you describe it in the future there is not a mismatch. If you state it in the present there is a misalignment and your mind starts to seek ways to make it a reality. So create your North Star by using the present tense and from a psychological place that states you are already in your ideal job… just like the discussion you had with that good friend.

Take Note

Principle 3 teaches that north is the only direction worth moving towards. It is the place of your hopes, dreams and ambitions so use it to navigate your way. Beware dilution of your dreams and ambitions with 'today thinking' – the inner voice of practical reasoning. This is your aspiration and it needs to feel a stretch from where you are now. Following your North Star requires a daring spirit and confidence to take action. Ask all high achievers: they will tell you it is worth it.

Moving On

Congratulations. If you have completed all the activity steps so far, you now have a clear destination for your career, you know where you are going and it feels compelling. In the next principle we explore how badly you want to close the gap between where you are now and where you want to be. You have to want to change. No one, not even you, can bring about that change if you've already decided beforehand that it's not worth the effort. In the next principle we will be focusing on creating a pathway to your success.

"The difference between where you are now and where you want to be is... what you do!"

Unknown

PRINCIPLE

Step on the Path

Many people meander through their careers aimlessly and idly without a fixed direction, always at the mercy of the decisions of others. Like the serial non-completers of New Year resolutions they are often overheard talking about what they aspire to achieve, but that is where it ends. I am reminded of the story that describes people in their likeness to bones. The 'wish bones' are the dreamers who sit around, never taking any action and live in hope that one fine day their dream will come true. The 'jaw bones' grumble and moan about how difficult and rotten things are and expect someone else to take action. The 'back bones' however are the people who roll up their sleeves, and set about making something happen: they take action. They know that positive visioning alone will not create success. Every company and every community has its share of 'jaw bones', 'wish bones', and 'back bones', the question is when it comes to planning and managing your career success which type are you?

Have you got a North Star, but are not moving towards it so it remains as an unobtainable and ever distant fixed point in the future? Or are you the person who has the fortitude or gumption to take action towards the achievement of your goals and aspirations? Most people are great at creating elaborate plans, however, they then fail to execute and achieve them. Setting great intentions and taking no action is simply a waste of your time and energy. Abandoning the plan in tricky times is equally not a great strategy. Career planning does not need to be complicated to be powerfully effective. Once you identify where you are now and where you want to go, the next thing you need to do is to abandon detail planning and simply take one clear and decisive step in the right direction.

◎ The last sentence may trigger some of your autopilot thinking. As the Chinese Philosopher Lao-tzu is quoted as saying: "a journey of a thousand miles begins with a single step". All you have to do is take a step and when you have taken it then you simply take another one. The career success design approach being explored here is structured to enable you to take simple success driven action steps. What is powerful is that the steps you decide to take naturally encompass your present thinking, current experience, knowledge and situation. With every step forward, very quickly a momentum occurs and you find that you begin to form a career success pathway. The pathway takes you directly towards your aspiration.

Have you ever seen a series of dominoes placed in a line of intricate pattern? They are placed on their end and evenly spaced, when the first domino is knocked over all the dominoes start to topple in succession. It is an amazing sight to behold as the speed of the toppling dominoes gains momentum. Your one step will set into motion a series of events until your subsequent steps generate a tipping point of energy that will carry you like a wave towards your destination. Do not underestimate the power of just taking a step; small action steps have been known to change the world. Rosa Parks' action not to give up her seat on a Montgomery bus in 1955 lit the touchpaper for the American civil rights movement. Dame Anita Roddick, founder of the Body Shop, which was the leading ethical cosmetics retailer in the UK in the 80s and 90s, campaigned against animal testing in the production of cosmetics and introduced the benefits of natural ingredients such as jojoba oil, aloe vera and cocoa butter, which were at the time unheard of in the cosmetic industry. Dr Mo Ibrahim is changing the world's view of the African continent. He believes that given the land and resources Africa has at its disposal, the continent is able to feed itself and should also be able to help others. With good governance and leadership, agriculture and natural resources can be a source of economic growth. In 2007 he established the Mo Ibrahim Prize for Achievement in African Leadership, awarded to an African leader who governs well in terms of delivering security, health, education and economic development for their people, and who then also democratically transfer power to their successors. Steve Jobs and Steve Wozniac, founders of Apple, had a vision that has pioneered a series of revolutionary technologies and brought about the personal computer and smartphone revolution.

One of the most difficult things about achieving dreams, ambitions and goals whatever label you choose to give your aspirations, is managing the discipline of persistent action and the patience required to see the vision into reality.

If you have completed the activities in the preceding pages you already have the essential ingredients for any career success mapmaker: where are you at present; identify the gap between your present and your North Star; then identify your first step and any obstacles (▲) that may appear on your path.

Career success map

Stepping On the Path

(A) Knowing that small decisive actions can lead to big results, pause for a moment and write down *one* small thing you can do *today* to get you closer to your ideal career aspiration. The key word here is **today**, not tomorrow or next week. The goal setting graveyard is overflowing with success plans that have been sunk by great intentions. The importance is to act immediately and not lose the momentum that fuels the process of achievement.

Stop NOW! Do not proceed any further until something has popped into your mind on which you are going to take action. Just in case you are not very good at stopping or missed the importance of the question, here it is again slightly expanded: given that you know who you are, the journey it has taken to get you to this point in your career and you know what you want to achieve, what is the smallest action you can take that will move you in the right direction towards your career aspiration? Write it down. I may be coming across as being pushy here, but that is because this is the point where many goals and tasks fail to materialise and become reality. This is not about asking someone else's opinion it needs to come from within you. If you are experiencing resistance then read the next section on obstacles and then come back to the question.

The reason one action is recommended as opposed to two or three is that experience has shown that one item always feels more achievable than three or four, and reduces the desire to procrastinate. It is easier to achieve when you have a single focus. The power of focus is a precondition for every success you have experienced. If you can tie shoelaces, drive a car, play an instrument, use a computer, utilise a software application, even write your signature, at some point it will have required you to use your power of focus. This is what is being asked of you here – what action are you going to focus on until completion?

If you have answered the question and you have a clear action step, it's time to do a mini victory dance. I am being serious. Have you noticed how successful sports people, when they win an event, grin, punch the air or do a victory lap or dance? In London 2012 Olympics did you observe Mo Farah do the Mobot and Usain Bolt do the lightning bolt when they won their events? Notice how children cheer spontaneously at their achievements and how, in business, colleagues spontaneously congratulate each other when they win a significant order? I am a big fan of the victory dance. I do them all the time: they are psychologically powerful, inexpensive but brilliantly motivating. If you haven't got a success ritual create one now. Every time you successfully complete an action you then need to acknowledge and celebrate the fact, identify the next action and complete it. Remember the celebration can simply be your victory dance, Mobot equivalent; a long soak in the bath as opposed to taking your usual shower; savouring a chocolate biscuit instead of having a plain – whatever works for you. The idea is to create a simple but personally-identifiable ritual for your success. You do not need to mark your success lavishly, the importance is to consciously and proactively acknowledge to yourself you have completed the action and kept your promise to yourself.

Whenever we step on a pathway to success several things can happen. One of which is the part of you that wants to keep you safe and remaining in the status quo can begin its sabotaging strategy. If you've chosen a slightly bigger step than you would normally take then potential obstacles are likely to appear. Regardless of the source of the obstacle you need to be able to quickly recognise and respond to it when it appears so as not to be derailed or delayed. If you have a psychological reservoir of success stories which readily come to mind because you've been carrying out your success rituals, you are less likely to be blown off course and will find you are far more resilient. A dance a day will keep your obstacles away. For many people obstacles often generate an unfavourable psychological response that if allowed to blossom can lead to derailment. I, however, believe they are powerful allies and can be very useful if you know just how to unlock their secrets.

The obstacle may be the path.

Have you ever hit a metaphorical brick wall? You have set a clear intention, created a plan, having taken into account all the possible variables, and then out of the blue an unforeseen blockage presented itself that stopped you in your tracks or stalled progress. The question is what do you do when faced with such an obstacle? Buddhist teaching reminds us that the obstacle *is* the path. Learning, growth and evolution comes from how we tackle our brick walls. Most people tell you they are 'achievement orientated', 'outcome focused' and/or 'goal centred' and they pride themselves on overcoming adversity. However it's when an obstacle presents itself that we see the truth within the statement. If you want something badly enough do you obliterate the brick wall, set about dismantling it brick by brick or turn around and walk in the other direction? Typically what occurs is if you are not committed to the chosen direction or action, you quickly give up or make excuses at the first sight of difficulty. Why do many career plans fail? Often it is because the goal is not magnetic and the individual is not committed or passionate about taking the necessary actions to achieve their plan. I encourage you to question: what if brick walls are your 'allies' and they show up to challenge you and to see if you want something badly enough? What if they are simply catalysts to significant change? When recruiting new staff a question that will always be posed in the recruitment and selection interview by managers and directors is a question about how you overcame an obstacle. The reason the question is asked so often is that how you tackle difficulties reveals a lot about who you are and whether you have gold medal success thinking.

Have you ever noticed those individuals that are supportive in their language at the start of a new initiative, however as you start to move towards the goal their jawbone and wishbone mindset presents itself and resistance obstacles are presented? They eat away until they have created a wall so big that you start to question the wisdom of taking on the initiative in the first place. Perhaps you are one of these people? When creating your career success plan this behaviour will kill your career aspiration. Obstacle blitzing has the potential to become a value asset to you if you learn to recognise them, fully appreciate and then optimise them to support you in achieving your goals. There is a famous parable from an unknown author that illustrates the point:

The obstacle in our path

In ancient times, a King had a boulder placed on a roadway. Then he hid himself and watched to see if anyone would remove the huge rock. Some of the King's wealthiest merchants and courtiers came by and simply walked around it. Many loudly blamed the King for not keeping the roads clear, but none did anything about getting the stone out of the way. Then a peasant came along carrying a load of vegetables. Upon approaching the boulder, the peasant laid down his burden and tried to move the stone to the side of the road. After much pushing and straining, he finally succeeded. After the peasant picked back up his load of vegetables, he noticed a purse lying in the road where the boulder had been. The purse contained many gold coins and a note from the King indicating that the gold was for the person who removed the boulder from the roadway. The peasant learned what many of us never understand: every obstacle presents an opportunity to improve our condition. The King learnt much about his wealthiest courtiers and merchants as well as about that particular peasant.

The success of the civil rights movement, anti-apartheid struggle, the suffragette movement and Edison's pursuit of electric light are powerful examples of boulder removal. Individuals focused on a destination and the overcoming of adversity obstacles to achieve success and create improvements that have empowered and created change for generations. It is through trials and tribulations that we can acquire new personal insights as well as notice the stuff that really matters. There is always learning within adversity and there is always a lesson to be learned that will take you to another level, even if at the time you cannot possibly entertain such a possibility. Hindsight and reflection can be great teachers.

So what is the wall? It's a metaphor that represents our bricks of concern, anything or anyone that generates a loss of focus, a feeling as though it is impenetrable, unrelenting or unyielding, something that stops us in our tracks, has us questioning whether we should proceed. The wall is not universal in nature, it varies in size and density and for each and every one of us it can be different. There are those people who attract walls; an event happens which then attracts other boulders until it becomes a meteor shower of rubble creating a wall, which stops them in their tracks.

The thing about brick walls is that they are highly personal. What is perceived as a wall by one person isn't necessarily a wall to another. As you are aware from the discussion on autopilot thinking, we all see the world through the filter of our own experiences. The filter is dependent upon a myriad of factors which include not only our autopilot thinking but also past experiences, personality, gender, socialisation, education, culture, so on and so forth. As a consequence there is no universal one-size-fits-all approach to resolving or overcoming obstacles.

Differing personalities approach their brick wall management differently. The type of personality that likes to be in charge, be in control, who is a highly-opinionated, big picture thinker and is typically not a broad thinker, will want to find strategies that very quickly annihilate the brick wall to achieve the goal so as to move on to the next challenge in hand. The logical and practical individual, who has good attention to detail, is analytical in nature, possessing expert in-depth knowledge in their field of expertise, who prefers everything around them to be in an orderly fashion, would want to loosen each brick carefully. Having examined every brick carefully until they have a full understanding of the whole wall, only then will they design the perfect plan to dismantle it. The individual whose focus is achieving results as part of a team will seek to ensure that the wall is not causing conflict or disharmony for others and to achieve a solution that benefits everyone equally. In their drive to want to be accommodating to the needs of others they are likely to put their brick wall needs secondary or to avoid dealing with the wall at all in case it causes harm. Of course the esoteric and Zen individual would acknowledge the presence of the wall, thank it for presenting itself then seek to be at one with it in order to raise their vibrations and walk effortlessly through it! Enough of the brick wall metaphor, I am sure you understand the message – obstacles present themselves. How you tackle and resolve them is unique to you. However there are opportunities to improve your creativity and innovation, to learn, grow or perhaps strengthen your skills and expertise. Obstacles are an opportunity to improve our condition.

Ⓐ If you didn't answer the question earlier then it's time to take action now and complete it: **What is the smallest action you can take immediately that will move you towards your North Star career aspiration? Write it down.**

Remember the 'right deadline law'. We all know that goals should have deadlines and yet we often forget to remember to apply them to personal goal setting. Any task or goal takes as much time as you allow it to take. By setting non-negotiable deadlines for yourself on every activity, your results will take off like a rocket into space. You are asked to identify the smallest action you can take NOW to move you towards your aspiration. If you genuinely can't identify an action step you can take today then aim to do it by tomorrow or the next day. If you are looking beyond three days to take an action then the step is too big. Break it down.

Let me share an example. In 2009 I had a career aspiration to become a published author. Writing a book felt like a big ask of myself. Also I wasn't confident anyone would want to read anything that I wrote. Despite repeated requests from clients about where my material can be found, I still had a doubt that questioned could I be a successful author? So using the career management success map one step approach I've just described this is what I did:

Step 1 I wrote a 500 word article.
Only when it was finished did I identify step 2.
I had an article and it needed a home.

Step 2 I researched online where I could publish it for free.

Step 3 I then opened an ezine.com account using a pseudonym.
It took me a few minutes to open the account.

Step 4 I published the article and tracked its results.
Steps 1 to 4 took me a total of a week! Three days of which was ezine.com article submission process.

Step 5   I repeated steps 1 and 4, five times.

Over 10,000 hits on my articles gave me confidence that I had something to say to a wider audience and not just those who were paying for my services.

Step 6   I wrote the first chapter of a book.

Step 7   I wrote chapter two, and the rest as they say is history.

I have subsequently authored several books and numerous articles. Were there any boulders? Absolutely, they included my irrational fears, the critical comments of one individual that I shared an article with and switching off my perfectionist desire to keep editing. As soon as I recognised them popping up at each step of the way, I simply acknowledged and dissolved them in order to move forward. I held myself to account keeping the overall aspiration in mind and only creating a step after I'd completed a step, carrying out my victory dance at each completion. When I got my first commission cheque from the publisher of my first book I danced, sang and then telephoned all my friends and family excitedly.

My example summarised:

Career success map

Present	Obstacles (▲)	Future
Unpublished author	Fear	Be a published author by
Creator of numerous course notes read by 1000s of participants.	Negative inner dialogue	December 2010
Author of a significant number of book reviews.	Critical friend	
	Time poor	
	Perfectionist	

Now Action

Write a 500 word article in the next seven days

Ⓐ Once you have identified the first small step that moves you in the direction of your aspiration, answer these supplementary questions: what is a possible boulder between this point and the success of this first action step that may stop you achieving this step? What will you do to roll the boulder out of the way? This does not need to be a detailed activity. Its purpose is to encourage you to notice any interference and then take action.

Take Note

Principle 4 teaches the importance of moving beyond conceptualisation, positive visioning and planning to take forward-moving action. The art is to benchmark each step against whether it moves you northwards and motivates you to completion. Your goals will never fail you, only implementation can do that. For example if your goal is to be a maths teacher will studying geography be beneficial? If you want to be a Sales and Marketing Director will freelancing at a PR agency get you to your destination? If the answer is no then don't take that step, decline the offer. In a tough job market, I recognise that not everybody has the luxury of turning down work. However settling for a job that moves you away from what you aspire to do and in most likelihood you will end up hating, poses risks that can negatively affect your career. Anything that visibly taints your attitude towards work and colleagues, or typecasts you into a job role that can be hard to break free from when you're ready to move is not a good move. Take steps, however small, that keep you moving north. With every completed step you know you are achieving.

Take Action Now

1. Take a blank sheet of paper and design your personalised map.

2. Plot your first action step and any obstacles that you think may attempt to slow you down.

Moving On

You know yourself, where you are heading, your first step on the path, which feels compelling, and you are aware of possible obstacles. What else does your career success strategy need? In the next chapter we add several essential plug-ins.

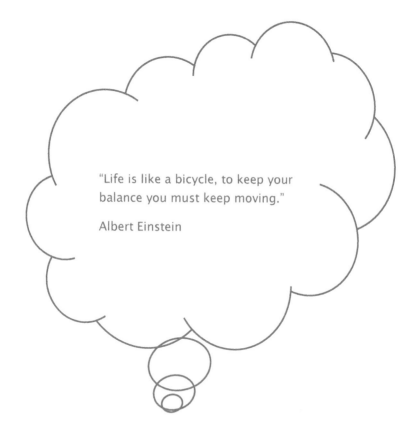

"Life is like a bicycle, to keep your balance you must keep moving."

Albert Einstein

PRINCIPLE

Plug in to Action

Having a strategic career management plan on its own is not enough when it comes to career success. As you increase steps along your pathway you will arrive at a point where external actions or communications become necessary. Where an opportunity presents itself or you find yourself in a conversation with a key person of influence. It is therefore vital that you are ready to meet the challenge. Having designed your career management strategic plan there are essential plug-ins that you also need to consider if your plan has not addressed them already. In computing, a plug-in is a component that adds specific capabilities to a wider application. It enables customisation and allows for additional features. Career success plug-ins are no different, they contain essential additions to your plan to ensure your career management strategy is achieved. They can be influenced by many variables, such as what is trending in your sector, the need for specific skills updating to stay current or key recruitment and selection essentials. The three standard career plug-ins for every professional would include:

Plug–in 1: Career Branding

Have you noticed how branding has become the face of business? Companies interact and influence us on a daily basis through their brands. Do you always buy a certain series of brand items in the supermarket? Do you prefer to wear a certain clothes label, perfume or aftershave? Do you aspire to have a certain product or accessory? Do you notice what labels others are wearing? If so you are branded. A brand can be defined as the unique identity of a specific product, service or business. It is whatever makes an entity definable and recognisable and once experienced it leaves an indelible impression that is uniquely distinguishable. Just like a business or your favourite product or service, your brand is an essential element of your career development strategy and for your personal marketing.

Personal branding is all around you. Nearly every celebrity, politician or athlete has a mechanism to communicate and promote their brand, for example most have personal websites, twitter feeds and/or a blog. A personal brand gives you the ability to stand out in a sea of similar products. In essence, it supports you in marketing yourself as something different from the rest of the pack. Remember the interview question where candidates give a generic answer thinking it is a good response? In a competitive market how do you stand out from the crowd? In a business bonus culture how can you stand out from your colleague when you are both achieving your performance targets and the bonus pot is constrained? If seeking internal promotion, why should you be chosen over someone else? Unless you can differentiate yourself from your competitors you are at the mercy of only achieving if others perform less favourably.

Which do you prefer: Coca-Cola® or Pepsi®? They are similar products, nearly identical in chemical composition, yet people routinely display strong preferences for one or the other. It is simply the branding that differentiates their uniqueness and informs your preference not the taste. Neuroscience researchers have found that knowing what brand you are buying can strongly influence your preferences as they take over brain circuits involved with memory, decision-making, reward and self-image. For example, when researchers monitored the brain scans of people who were given an anonymous taste test of Coca-Cola® and Pepsi®, i.e. the participants did not know which brand of cola they were tasting, participants were evenly split and quite neutral as to which drink they preferred. However when the same people were told what they were drinking, known as a brand-cued taste test, the results were dramatic. The researchers observed and measured very different brain activity and responses. When participants were told the brand before tasting, three out of four people stated they preferred Coke. The areas linked to brand loyalty overrode their original preferences.[9]

In big business the branding strategy is integral in guiding companies to achieve goals and is considered vital for business success. Likewise career branding is an important aspect of your career success design strategy, as it will support you in not only showcasing who you are, but also ensuring that the individuals and companies with whom you seek to develop a relationship prefer you to another candidate or applicant. Personal career brands are about creating an identity by which people can recognise you and have a positive psychological association. It is perhaps worth noting, that although the words are often used interchangeably, branding and advertising are not the same thing. Personal branding is all about differentiation. It helps define who you are in the eyes of others, it showcases your talent and signposts people to what sets you apart from others and why you should be considered above everyone else. You have the power to influence the perceptions others have of you by your actions, achievements and how you choose to present yourself. The mistake people often make is waiting until they are looking for a new job or for a career change to consider their personal brand. Be clear, a brand is not an instantaneous creation; it takes time to build.

Plug-ins for your career brand

(1) Brand Profile

Career branding is not about making you feel good, its aim is to differentiate you from the competition and to showcase how you bring more value to your work and to the target market that you seek to serve. Your career brand will clearly communicate your individuality to the people who need to know about you. As a part of your career success design strategy, career branding will act as a filter that helps you make decisions that are consistent with who you are and what you are seeking to achieve. How do you brand yourself?

- Know thyself – the start of any branding journey is brand definition. The service being branded is you.

- Identify your ideal employer or client – this is your target market. The more you can research and find out about them the better. What do they consider as being important, who are their high-flyers?

- Design your brand profile. Gathering all the information you have gathered from the activities in this book, the knowledge you have about future trends, and your ideal employer create a succinct statement of your unique promise of value.

◎ Knowing what you know about yourself and what you want to achieve. What are three things that you do that can deliver value to your existing or future employer? Once you have generated some ideas you then need to create a professional story.

(2) Tell a professional story

Once you have clarified your brand (the indelible you), the next step is to ensure it is effectively communicated. One of the oldest tools for telling others about who you are is the CV. Let's be clear, you most definitely need a good CV, however on its own it is no longer enough. In this digital age, you require both a print profile (CV) and an online profile. It is no longer unusual for prospective employers to 'Google' the names of prospective job candidates and base their initial candidate screening decisions on the quality of what they find. Research carried out by several large UK recruitment firms over the past two years reveals consistent patterns – not only do employers use online screening, but they disregard candidates on the content that they find on social networking sites. Examples cited for non-selection or shortlisting include:

• The candidate lied about their qualifications.

• Candidate makes discriminatory comments.

• They found posted content about the candidate revealing behaviour associated with excessive drinking, usage of drugs or they were observed in provocative or inappropriate photographs.

• Candidate has bad-mouthed their current or previous employer and/or clients.

The lesson here is – not only does your brand need to have a strong online presence it needs to present you in a positive light.

 **A suggested activity**

Put your name into a search engine and see what it reveals. If you are not happy with what you find or you would not be content for a future employer or client to see what you have found, clean up your profile. Equally if you cannot be found or are lost in a sea of other people with whom you share your name then you need to create a clear and strong profile. Creating an online profile allows you to create a space where you can showcase your expertise. Your online profile needs to support your application or client proposal. It needs to reassure and portray a professional image; ideally it should be supplemented with references from colleagues, clients and/or managers. Always remember prospective employers can also see your friends whom you have less influence over.

Online Profile Rules of Thumb

- Keep personal and professional separate – you want prospective employers, staff or colleagues to find what you want them to see, and to ensure that what they are viewing is appropriate.

- Build a professional online profile – there exist several business professional profiling and networking sites, by far the most popular is LinkedIn. This site is widely used by HR professionals, headhunters and recruiters. You need a presence here. In addition, when your name is put into a search engine LinkedIn profiles are optimised: they appear on the front pages of Google search engine lists. If proactively job searching use the summary section to present your promise of value.

- Social media such as Facebook/Twitter/Myspace is evolving from being just about social networking, to becoming a space for personal marketing. If you have a presence here then make sure it is professional. People have fallen foul of the Facebook phenomena of thinking that what is shared here is invisible.

- Visual impact – when building your online profile it is not uncommon to include a photograph. Give some thought to the image that you choose, think of your photo as your logo. A good quality headshot is recommended. Look positive and remember the old adage – 'a picture says a thousand words', it is said that appearance represents 55% of your influencing power.

CV Profile Rules of Thumb

A CV is in reality a marketing document, it is a sales pitch and a covering letter is a sales pitch for your CV. There is a lot of good and free CV advice available online. My colleagues and I see hundreds of CVs per year and it still beggars belief that despite the plethora of information available on the subject people still get this very badly wrong. Here are some CV essentials:

- **Keep it short and clear**: Before you start, choose the right structure for your CV. It should normally not exceed two pages in length unless you have a very long career, are a contractor or the recruiter asks for a longer CV. Five page CVs very rarely ever get read!

- **Most recent first**: Put your employment history in date order, starting with the most recent first. Avoid leaving any gaps. Don't go into detail about positions you held over ten years ago.

- **Showcase your achievements:** You can have a great brand, but if no one knows about it, you are not going to have very much success. Presenting your achievements is essential. It is not a time for modesty – if you have achieved something, promote it. Include a series of concise bullet points under the heading Achievements with each role you are showcasing. A trap that many people fall into, is presenting job functions as achievements. For example "managed a team of ten people". This is not an achievement unless you turned a poor performing team around, or led the team to achieve an almost unbelievable outcome. At all times focus on the reader, you are unlikely to be able to present everything you have done in your career on two or three pages, therefore pick out the most relevant information to share. If your achievement can support your points of value then even better.

- **Make it look good**: Clear, attractive presentation is important if your CV is to stand out. Ensure that it's uncluttered, with key points that are easy to spot. Use a sensible size font, using a size eight font and extending the page margins so you can squeeze more information on the page is not attractive and is likely to have your CV passed over. CVs often get photocopied or printed in black and white, so remove any desire on your part for colour or the inclusion of a photo unless requested.

- **Breathe some life into it**: Remember the employer wants a sense of the kind of person you are, as well as what you can do. Ask yourself "What does this CV say about me?" Leverage the use of a personal profile to describe who you are. A profile is a profile summary and not a 'please give me a job' begging request.

- **Adapt it**: Don't use the same CV every time. Tailor your CV to suit the job you're applying for. It isn't a case of one-size-fits-all. At all times make it relevant to the reader. For example including you have a clean driving licence when applying for a role where you will never be required to drive is taking up valuable space and adding no value. Ensure it showcases that you can do the job, add value and is not just focused on telling a story about your past. When you have written each section ask yourself the 'so what?' question as it relates to the person reading your CV.

- **Online profile**: Include in your address section your LinkedIn profile URL or a web address to your online personal profile or website if you have one.

- **Be truthful:** Although you obviously want to present yourself well, don't go too far and embellish the truth. It can easily backfire on you, particularly when it is checked against your online profile.

Plug–in 2: Network Building

A network is simply a series of relationships and connections that exist between a group of people. Effective networks are those where people have mutual respect and a foundation that supports exchange. For example, it is a myth to think all jobs are advertised, more often or not opportunities arise out of a strong network. The quality of which can also reveal much about who you are. Have you ever been asked at interview: how did you find out about this job? Then as the interviewer moves through your career history the question is asked again about each successive job change?

If you have watched the TV programme *The Apprentice*, in the latter round candidates are interviewed by senior company directors. As they interrogate candidates and their CVs there is an underlying value being explored – are you just looking for a job or are you seeking to add value to the company? Statements such as "I'm a hard worker" do not inspire an interviewer. Dr. Margaret Mountford who took part in the early series of the UK version of the programme shared the following valid points of view when interviewed for a business article: "The candidate who only finds each successive job from generic advertisements or postings typically hasn't got a career strategy or hasn't worked out what he or she wants to do and where he or she would like to do it. They are just looking for a job; often any job. For an employer it probably means that he or she isn't particularly eager to work for you and will only stay until something else comes along". Ouch! You may not like the message, but ask yourself if it rings true for you or anyone you know.

Career high-flyers will often describe finding their first few jobs on job boards, general postings, and online listings or at job fairs. However by the time they get to job four or five the opportunities are finding them. If you've had several jobs and someone you previously worked with or for, hasn't introduced you into a job or told a headhunter you are an ideal candidate, then that is a red flag. It indicates that not only have you not built effective professional relationships, but most importantly you haven't demonstrated a level of competence that made someone go out of their way to recommend you or bring you into their organisation. Personal recommendation is THE best reference you can ever have.

Networking Rules of Thumb

- Develop great relationship-building habits. The time to build a network is when you are seeking nothing in return not when you are chasing the next job.

- Old-school networkers are typically transactional, focused on acquiring relationships based solely on what other people can do for them. They end up building a lot of connections not a network. A successful network is built on a foundation of trust, respect, mutual collaboration and exchange.

- LinkedIn is geared to help you build an online networking platform. Used effectively it can be a useful plug-in to your career success strategy. For example, helpful networks are about exchange, whether it is providing advice, expertise, information or experiences. By joining groups, of which there are over one million on LinkedIn, these informal communities formed around industries, professions and themes enable you to observe what is current and to contribute to relevant debate. You can showcase your knowledge and expertise through posing and answering questions, spot trends, make new connections and find new opportunities. If you are not active within your network then you are missing out.

- Build a well-rounded and diverse network on and offline. Remember it is the quality of your network, not the quantity of members that is important. For example who fulfils the all-important mentoring and coaching role for you? Who are the subject matter experts to whom you can refer? Who acts as a natural connector or ideas generator? Who can act as a testimonial of the quality of what you deliver? Who have you supported? If you review your current network how balanced and diverse is it?

- You do not own a network and you cannot own the relationships. What a network does is act as a potential collaborative ally. To create a truly helpful network it needs to be authentic and reflect you. The people you associate and network with will create an impression about who you are. However it is the 'weak ties' associated with your network that can be leveraged to great effect in finding your next career opportunity. Weak ties are the relationships we have with people outside our own social networks. Economic sociologist Mark Granovetter[10] was one of the first people to consider the use of social networks in understanding how information is spread. In his seminal 1973 paper, 'The Strength of Weak Ties', where he asked a random sample of professionals how they had found their new job he revealed that 82% of them had acquired it through the individuals they interact with infrequently rather than their close personal contacts. He referred to these more distant connections as 'weak ties'. Subsequent studies into social networking reinforce the principle of his findings.[11] As weak ties sit outside of your inner circle there is a greater likelihood that a weak tie will be exposed to a range of new career opportunities that you would otherwise miss.

**Social Networking Graph.
Source Facebook Data (2012)**

A weak tie acquaintance whose job and background is identical to yours is unlikely to add any value to you. The value lies in having weak ties who are from a different background or move in different circles and your ability to access them through your strong ties or your online networking platform. At the risk of appearing yet again as a promoter of LinkedIn, this highly respected business platform is a good current example of how you can access your strong and weak ties. It enables you to post requests, questions and comments to a very wide circle of contacts.

Plug-in 3: Rewards and Remuneration

Remuneration is the total compensation that you will earn for delivery of a specific job or service. It includes both monetary and, in some cases, supplementary benefits such as healthcare, holidays, bonuses, travel, training and development. It is simply a contractual exchange of 'tokens' for your contribution that allows you to live your life.

Plug-ins for your Reward and Remuneration

(1) Know your needs and wants

When designing your career strategy you need to gain clarity on your needs and wants. Calculate what you need in terms of income in order to make your aspiration viable. Be clear about what you need to thrive. If you were seeking to borrow a significant sum of money from a bank they would ask you to complete a budget planner. As part of your career strategy it is strongly suggested you carry out this exercise. What does it genuinely cost to maintain your life today and what will it cost for where you want your life to be several years from now? This is not a finger in the air take a guess exercise, this information is vital in aiding your decision on whether to apply for a post or developing a negotiating plan for your remuneration package when you are offered the job of your dreams. Most people when they carry out this exercise outline a financial range; the sum they cannot go below, this is your break even point, no matter how great the job you will not be able to meet your commitments if you accept that package point. This is complimented by an aspirational level where you are clear about what remuneration package you need to live your best at work and out-of-work life.

Ⓐ Create your remuneration and reward profile:

```
┌─────────────────────────────────────────────┐
│           Remuneration Profile              │
│                                             │
│   Salary:        40 L                        │
│                                             │
│   Annual leave:   25                         │
│                                             │
│   Working hours:     40                       │
│                                             │
│   Benefit requirements:   10 - 15 %          │
│     health, phone, accidental cover,        │
│                    dental                    │
└─────────────────────────────────────────────┘
```

(2) Do your research

Carry out some desk research and identify the salaries and benefit packages on offer for similar roles that you are interested in. It is vitally important to keep a watchful eye on remuneration levels in your sector so that you always know the average industry sector value for your professional skills. A good source for this information is industry sector recruitment sites, professional journals, and online salary checkers, or of course asking your network. If you find yourself in a remuneration negotiation position this knowledge is invaluable as you can position yourself from a place of strength not ignorance.

Take Note

Only three career plug-ins have been presented here, you may have identified several more that are more relevant to your situation. Plug-ins are designed to create important customisation to your career management strategy. They focus you on what you need to pay attention to in order to succeed. For example, developing a strong network made up of former colleagues, employees suppliers, vendors or even a competitor is a powerful resource plug-in to try to get an introduction to somebody who can offer some insight about what it's like to work for the company you're seeking to work in. Principle 5 teaches don't be constrained, add or subtract plug-ins as necessary to create your personalised success plan.

Take Action Now

Create a set of powerful plug-ins that supports your career management strategy.

Moving On

Given where you are now you may feel you have acquired several other areas of thinking that may generate additional action steps towards your North Star. The rule remains the same, stay focused – identify one step only, take action, achieve, celebrate and then take another step. The speed at which you travel is determined by you; five victory dances in one week is great, one victory dance every two weeks is also fine. The key thing is to take inspired action and move towards your aspiration.

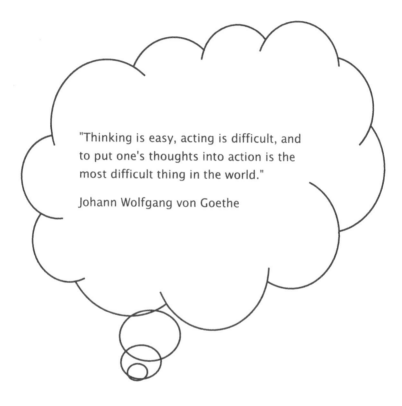

"Thinking is easy, acting is difficult, and to put one's thoughts into action is the most difficult thing in the world."

Johann Wolfgang von Goethe

Career Success by Design

As we near the end of our journey it's time to pull everything together into a coherent format. The concepts in this book are very simple, dare I say it, and they are also not rocket science. However we all know that just because something is simple it doesn't mean that it's easy. The five principles presented throughout this book have taken you on a journey to create a simple yet personalised map that takes you from where you are now to where you aspire to be. The process has been one of mindfulness and focusing on one step at a time. Master planners, multi-taskers or those who enjoy crafting detailed project plans may well struggle with the concept of only identifying and focusing on 'one step at a time' career planning. I speak from a place of knowing, as I love to create detailed plans and spreadsheets. Detailed planning with contingency plans and risk assessments has its place, however, it's not here.

The world of work is changing rapidly, the discipline outlined to manage your career in these ever-changing times, although it may feel counter-intuitive, is sound and more importantly it works. Take one step in the right direction and follow the course until you complete it. Success loves speed so maintain a sense of urgency and complete each action as quickly as you are realistically able. Amongst the many options that may present themselves to you choose just one direction and take action straight away whilst your intent is strong. If your goal is important to you, beware the temptation to multi-task, procrastinate, give yourself excuses or digress from your path, as many people are prone to do. The tiny gap between making your decision and taking action is the time when what seems impossible becomes possible. It is the point at which you choose not to settle for mediocrity; it's the intersection between your success and failure in a task. Results are everything – they enable you to develop a narrative for yourself and others that conveys how successful you are and how successful you feel. There is no better way to develop a career management success narrative than to have designed and successfully walked down a pathway of success. If you can master these five career management principles you will find that, like the dominoes I mentioned earlier, following the approach leads to rapid and very achievable personal success.

As you have journeyed through these pages, the following career map has underpinned each step of information that you have collated:

Career Success Map

Ⓐ Now it is time for you to take the map concept one step further and create a strategy canvas for your career. This is a visual chart or storyboard comprising of five central building blocks that summarise your reflections and clarify the actions that you need to undertake. It acts as a blueprint capturing and informing the narrative of your route to actionable success for your career management strategy. If you have undertaken the exercises and gained several insights I am encouraging you to complete this final stage and to design your career canvas.

The career canvas building blocks

Block 1 focuses on the
Present

The questions it answers are:
- What's trending for you?
- What do you love to do?
- What are you bringing to the party?
- What new skills do you require for the future?

Block 2 focuses on the
North Star

The questions it answers are:
- What do you really want?
- Is there a gap between what you want and where you are now?

Block 3 focuses on
Plug-ins

The questions it answers are:
- Does your career brand need attention?
- How effective is your network?
- Is your reward and remuneration profile as you would like it?
- What's trending that you need to consider?

Block 4 focuses on
Obstacles

The question it answers is:
- What are your blockers, obstacles or things that will cause you to stumble?

Block 5 focuses on

The questions it answers are:
- What is the smallest action that you can undertake now to move you towards the direction of your aspiration?
- Space to capture and track stepped progress.

The Career Canvas

Present	North Star	Plug-ins
	Obstacles	
Now Action		

Example 1 of a completed Career Canvas

A three-month canvas from one of our 2012 programme participants.

Present	North Star	Plug-ins
Great network in my sector. Work collaboratively in partnerships. Strong fundraising ability. Deliver against targets Possess youth and community management experience along with the utilisation of 'wraparound' models of care for each child. Good reputation for process and project management.	To be a Director level contributor to a business where sport is used as a mechanism to inspire and develop excluded young people. Work in a company with the values & philosophy of Kids Company. Have a Liberty and Justice Human Rights Award.	Government policy. National public sector funding strategy. PR – Increase visibility within my sector.

Obstacles
Lack confidence when presenting at Board level.
Not very good in political situations, prefer direct and plain speaking.
Currently left to my own devices a more senior position will mean less hands-on in programme design.

Now Actions
Identify a senior manager or director from Kids Company and approach them to become my mentor. (Completed 15 Aug) ☺
Appointment made for meeting at Kids Company to discuss mentoring or collaborative working – (Completed 25ᵗʰ Sept) ☺
NOW: Updating CV in preparation for meeting by 21ˢᵗ Sept

Outcome: nine-month review:
- Moved into a more senior leadership & management role in a children's charity.

- Working closely on a flagship project with two of the board trustees who act as project sponsors. A quarterly requirement is to present project updates to the main board of directors and influence the strategic direction of the initiative.

Example 2 of a completed Career Canvas

A three-month canvas from one of our 2011 programme participants.

Present	North Star	Plug-ins
Trending: Big Data Integration storage analytics Digital Universe 2020 Managed several cost reduction programmes. Lead and manage a successful team in a changing and challenging environment. Love the challenge of meeting client needs whilst generating exciting revenues.	To lead a business transformation and change programme at Board level in the IT or Telco sector	Profile Network building

	Obstacles Seen as a specialist not generalist CV does not demonstrate board level experience Network at my peer level EMEA experience

Now Actions

Talk to a headhunter about my CV and personal marketing (Complete) ☺

Talk to HR about my career development options (Complete) ☺

NOW: Identify a strategic networking space and build new relationships

Outcome: twelve-month review:
- Gained sponsorship from a board director in my company who is acting as my mentor.
- Attended internal soft skills training courses.

- Sitting on the board of a local charity gaining board level experience.
- Now an active member of two networking groups.

Health Warning

It would be very remiss of me not to inform you that having a career management success plan does have a little bit of a downside. "The only thing constant is change" - this saying is as true today as when Heraclitus first said it over 2,500 years ago. If you are standing still or attempting to maintain the status quo, you are in reality actually slipping backwards. Life today is like a stream that is flowing slowly against you, to stand still in the same place you will find you nevertheless have to occasionally step forward. To get ahead, thrive and stay ahead you must move forward proactively, consistently and regularly. Here lies the cost to having a career management success strategy that is working. You may find you need to join a 'new club'. The successful change club! The more successful you become and move forward, the less likely you will be able to join in the general moaning or blaming conversations of others. Colleagues and friends will start to notice that there is a change in your appearance as you act in alignment with your brand. They will notice your reluctance to complain, the way in which you take learning from every situation and as you take repeated action and achieve success they will begin to question why. Without a doubt the more of a success mindset you create, reinforced by your success ritual such as the victory dance, the more fulfilled you will feel and the greater the pull of your higher or strategic vision. Should you find yourself in this situation here are some of the career success tips that you have acquired and that you may want to share with your colleagues and friends:

1. Own your career

It is up to you to make your career aspirations happen. Take charge, it is not your employer, manager or colleague's responsibility. Jawboning is a noisy distraction that sabotages progress and keeps you where you are.

2. Right place, right time

Being in the right place at the right time is no longer enough. In a competitive marketplace you need direction, a coherent brand, and to be adaptive in your actions. Be courageous and unconventional from time to time. Staying in your comfort zone keeps you out of the success lane. Scaffold yourself a plan. Scaffolding has its roots in the study of human behaviour. It is the approach taken to support and build on prior knowledge and internalise new information to achieve a development outcome.

3. Be an expert in what you choose to do or be

Ensure you have the essential knowledge and skills in place to create credibility and use this as a platform from which to build your core areas of expertise. Be stunningly good at what you do and have people talk about your expertise with confidence. This will differentiate you from others and they are more likely to recommend you when they get the call from the headhunter in the future.

4. Life-long learning

Success going forward will require continuous development and learning. Pay attention to what is trending in your area of expertise and ensure you keep your professional and transversal skills updated. Be curious and take advantage of situations that afford you new learning. Attention is one of your most powerful tools, find playful ways to enhance it and reduce any activities that diffuse it.

5. Generate new ideas and actively seek different experiences

Ideas and new experiences create new neural networks which

when explored wire to different experiences. When those networks are activated, they trigger the firing of networks responsible for thinking and behaving. The repeated firing causes physical changes in the structure of the brain, and change the experience of the world you are creating. You evolve through this process.

6. **Expect obstacles and walls**

Any goal, plan or objective you set is likely to throw up some obstacles. You cannot have a contingency plan for them all. Know that they may occur and honour the brick wall. If you can hold the precept that obstacles exist for a purpose, be proactive in identifying the learning that obstacles bring and use these to overcome the challenge.

7. **Make an indelible impression**

Having a clear personal brand means you know who you are, what is important and you communicate it through everything that you do and say. Your outer appearance and non-verbal behaviours communicate to your target market key aspects of who you are at first sight and on every touch point of contact with you.

8. **Be a confident and authentic networker.**

Relationships are essential to your future career success.

9. **Celebrate your achievements**

Carry out a victory dance a day and raise a toast to your success.

Final Comments

So there you have it. As we traverse these ever-changing times you are equipped with some new knowledge, tips and techniques that will stand you in good stead and support you in achieving your career goals and aspirations.

This career management strategy is not for everyone. It requires some initial effort on the part of the reader and in this instant gratification world the idea of taking patient steps towards a goal isn't very attractive. However at all times, you are in control of the speed of the steps. It works powerfully if you operate in a spirit of mindfulness, with an eye on your destination; each step you design will occur in response to the trends and events occurring around you.

I encourage you to take note that the odds that you'll succeed in achieving any of your goals without taking action are about the same as you thinking you can win the lottery without buying a ticket! I hand the baton over to you – be mindful, adaptive and keep your North Star in sight.

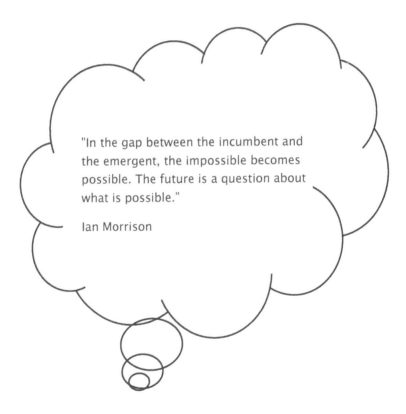

"In the gap between the incumbent and the emergent, the impossible becomes possible. The future is a question about what is possible."

Ian Morrison

References

Aaron, R. with Lacher, S. (2008) *Double your income doing what you love: Raymond Aaron's guide to power mentoring.* Wiley & Sons Inc, New Jersey.

Auter, D. (2010) *The Polarization of Job Opportunities in the U.S. Labor Market: Implications for Employment and Earnings.* MIT Department of Economics and National Bureau of Economic Research.

Bakshy, E. (2012) *Rethinking Information Diversity in Networks.* Facebook Data.

Barter, T. (April 2012) *Diversity and Performance.* McKinsey and Company.

CEDEFOP. *Future Skills Supply and Demand in Europe: Forecast 2012.* Luxembourg: Publications Office of the European Union, 2012.

Davies, A, Devin F, Gorbis, M. (2011) *Future Work Skills 2020.* Institute for the Future for University of Phoenix Research Institute.

Goleman, D. (1998) *Working with Emotional Intelligence.* Bloomsbury.

Granovetter, M. (1973) *The Strength of Weak Ties.* American Journal of Sociology.

Hebb, D.O. (1970) *The Organization of Behavior*. New York: Wiley & Sons.

McClure, S.M., Li, J. Tomlin, D., Cypert, K.S., Montague, L.M., and Montague, P.R. (2004) *Neural Correlates of Behavioral Preference for Culturally Familiar Drinks*. *Neuron*, Volume 44, Issue 2.

Ryde, R. (2007) *Thought Leadership: Moving Hearts and Minds*. Palgrave Macmillan.

World Assembly on Ageing 2002 (2001) *World Population Ageing: 1950-2050*. United Nations.

About the Author

Sue Liburd

A multi-award-winning businesswoman, with twenty-five years' experience in behavioural change management, human resource management and people development. Her purpose is to transform businesses and organisations through the development of their key people.

Underpinned with a Master's degree in Human Resource Management and Development, Postgraduate Diplomas in management, health, psychological trauma, behaviour, coaching and education. This former nurse, midwife, army officer, HR professional who went on to gain extensive experience in a number of senior management and board director level roles, has a proven track record of success. Leveraging her operational and board-level experience, she works internationally with directors, senior managers and their teams in companies of all sizes, across a diverse range of industry sectors, including complex international multi-sited corporations, local government, retail and community regeneration organisations. In addition to her client work where she advises, consults, facilitates and coaches, she is a business mentor, non-executive director and author of no-nonsense professional-development articles and publications.

Acknowledgments

I'm particularly grateful for the constructive feedback and comments on the manuscript provided by Sophie Constant, Barbara Gray-Murray and Linda Oola who worked through the manuscript and its exercises and who have taken action on their discoveries and insights. A thank you goes to John Cusack for his support and encouragement to submit my guidance into the written word, as well as for his timely comments and insights. Thanks to Karen Whelan, Executive coach and career management guide, not only for her feedback but also for her no nonsense comments in the earlier drafts. My brother Michael also gets a mention, for when he observed that the micro version had received over 10,000 hits online, suggesting I expand the discussion and turn it into a more substantial read. To my mentees and those individuals who have read my extended essays and/or experienced the journey in real time, I thank you. To those who have emailed and said "please can we have more", I hope this meets your needs. I also wish to thank Sage Blue's corporate clients who have purchased our executive coaching, training and facilitation services over the years and without whom I would not have gained this wealth of pragmatic experience.

Some of the readers' comments

"Once I started I couldn't stop. It was a bit like listening to a Pentecostal church service and personally relating to the testaments – Sue is talking about me!"

" It flowed so that each section set me up to read the next bit with the practical exercises arriving at the right time and I was equipped to do them."

"It all came together for me in the career success by design section combining my new insights with practical activities and it was especially here I saw the value of the Wake up and Smell the Coffee and The Art of Mindfulness chapters."

"I like the mix between the modern and ancient proverbs and wisdom."

"An intelligent and thought provoking read. I felt you were actually speaking to me directly"

"The exercises are quite telling first time round, you want to lie to yourself then realise it's you who will lose out"

"I really enjoyed reading/learning: I could identify at almost every level – stern but not in 'your face' a firm wake up call and smell the coffee kind of interaction!"

"There are almost two books in one – the theoretical book with tools and a practical book of exercises with some context for those who want to dive straight into action. Something for everyone in this time of change."

Notes

1   World Population Ageing: 1950-2050, United Nations, 2001. This
     report was prepared by the Population Division as a contribution to
     the 2002 World Assembly on Ageing.

2   The Office for National Statistics (ONS) is the UK's largest
     independent producer of official statistics and the recognised
     national statistical institute of the UK.

3   Cedefop undertakes various European level research activities. It
     produces regular skill supply and demand forecasts for Europe and
     analyses the potential labour market imbalances. Cedefop also
     investigates skill and competence needs in selected sectors and
     explores a common European approach to enterprise surveys on
     changing skill needs.

4   David Autor, MIT Department of Economics and National Bureau
     of Economic Research April 2010. The Polarization of Job
     Opportunities in the U.S. Labor Market Implications for
     Employment and Earnings.

5   Diversity and performance. McKinsey April 2012.

6   The 2012 IBM CEO Study, Leading Through Connections, explored
     how CEOs were responding to the complexity of increasingly
     interconnected organisations, markets, societies and governments.

7   Ryde, Robin (2007). Thought Leadership: Moving Hearts and
     Minds.

8   Donald Hebb, Ph.D., a Canadian neuropsychologist, presented a
     theory of learning and memory based on synaptic transmission in
     the central nervous system. According to Hebb's research, when we
     learn new information we change the relationship between neurons.

9   Samuel M. McClure, Jian Li· Damon Tomlin, Kim S. Cypert,
     Latané M. Montague and P. Read Montague. (2004). 'Neural

Correlates of Behavioral Preference for Culturally Familiar Drinks'. *Neuron*, volume 44, Issue 2.

[10] M. Granovetter. 'The Strength of Weak Ties'. *American Journal of Sociology*, 1973.

[11] Eytan Bakshy (2012). *Rethinking Information Diversity in Networks*. Facebook Data.

Lightning Source UK Ltd.
Milton Keynes UK
UKOW06f1912170414

230142UK00010B/40/P